THE PORTAGE POETRY SERIES

Series Titles

After the 8-Ball
Colleen Alles

Careful Cartography
Devon Bohm

Broken On the Wheel
Barbara Costas-Biggs

Sparks and Disperses
Cathleen Cohen

Holding My Selves Together: New and Selected Poems
Margaret Rozga

Lost and Found Departments
Heather Dubrow

Marginal Notes
Alfonso Brezmes

The Almost-Children
Cassondra Windwalker

Meditations of a Beast
Kristine Ong Muslim

Praise for
Colleen Alles

From the title of Colleen Alles's collection of poems, *After the 8-Ball*, to the concluding poem where the speaker searches for "the right word for the fullness of it all," reading these poems is a delight. There is much sweetness here, but also loss and uncertainty, and Alles has wisely organized this knowledge around those murky messages we find when we ask the magic little 8-ball to give us the answer we desire. Sometimes it does; sometimes it doesn't. So, too, with life. These are incredibly hospitable poems, inviting us into the poet's life the way Mary Oliver invites us to walk with her into the woods or William Stafford invites us to think about the meaning of life through his discovery of a dead deer. Her appreciation for the natural world, the complexities of motherhood, and her attempt to articulate the beauty and pain of relationships past and present make this a collection that offers insight from the ordinary, and hope, because, "who knows what might happen today?"

—Anita Skeen
Founding Director, RCAH Center for Poetry
Series Editor, Wheelbarrow Books

The "I" at the center of Colleen Alles's poems attends with precision to the presence of the lived world and also speaks to larger, invisible issues for which the magic 8-ball is a glib panacea. In "Three Words for Sunset" a mother consoles her son over a lost marble and herself for all that is coming. "I don't know how to say we may never find it." Birds, weather, thought, and relationships, always complicated. For me, *After the 8-Ball* had everything.

—Elizabeth Kerlikowske
Poetry Society of Michigan

After the 8-Ball is a beautiful, big-hearted, restless book of poems that linger on motherhood and marriage, the moon and Lake Michigan, walking and running, gratitude and hunger. Colleen Alles has given readers a true gift: language that adroitly captures what it's like to be alive in this world, a singular human in a human body, awash in memories, mourning, and the wistful, wondrous loneliness of everyday life. I love this book, and you will too.

—Amorak Huey
author of *Dad Jokes from Late in the Patriarchy*

In *After the 8-Ball*, desire lives alongside grief, love alongside memory, family alongside solitude. Colleen Alles plays with unlikely miracles here: a house that becomes a woman, the moon's reluctance to shine, the memories of tadpoles, the tantalizing answers of the Magic 8-Ball. Her poems remind us how difficult it can be to live in the worlds we have made for ourselves and "just how wondrous it is to be us." Should everyone read this beautiful book? As I see it, yes.

—W. Todd Kaneko
author of *This Is How the Bone Sings*

These poems are both the paper that bears invaluable missives and the paperweight that keeps them close at hand. How grateful I am to have spent quality time with a fellow traveler who asks—no sings to—"a pigeon to tell me the secret of how I could be Queen" and to a tree "What if I'm bound for the orchard?" and to a hound "What's the right word for the fullness of it all?" Here are some decidedly right words.

—Alison Swan
author of *A Fine Canopy*

With a clear eye and unique voice, Colleen Alles peers into life's mysteries like a seer. She knows the terrain—whether it embraces the grief on a menu or the longing of a young son who "wants to pull himself through/my walls—". Her poems never blink, never back down as they give witness to those small things that make us most alive. *After the 8-Ball* is a wise and remarkable collection.

—Linda Nemec Foster
author of *The Blue Divide, Talking Diamonds,*
and *Amber Necklace from Gdansk*

After the 8-Ball

Poems by

Colleen Alles

Cornerstone Press
Stevens Point, Wisconsin

Cornerstone Press, Stevens Point, Wisconsin 54481
Copyright © 2022 Colleen Alles

www.uwsp.edu/cornerstone

Printed in the United States of America by
Point Print and Design Studio, Stevens Point, Wisconsin 54481.

Library of Congress Control Number: 2021949399
ISBN: 978-1-7377390-3-6

Cornerstone Press titles are produced in courses and internships offered by the Department
of English at the University of Wisconsin–Stevens Point.

DIRECTOR & PUBLISHER   EXECUTIVE EDITOR   SENIOR EDITORS
Dr. Ross K. Tangedal   Jeff Snowbarger   Lexie Neeley & Monica Swinick

SENIOR PRESS ASSISTANT
Gavrielle McClung

STAFF
Rosie Acker, Megan Bittner, Rhiley Block, Jordan Boldt, Kala Buttke, Grace Dahl,
Camila Freund, Angela Green, Brett Hill, Cale Jacoby, Jaden Kerkhoff, Seth Kundinger,
Amanda Leibham, Pachia Moua, Dylan Potter, Cassie Ress, Annika Rice, Abbi Rohde,
Abbi Wasielewski, Bethany Webb, Maggie Weiland

For my family

Also by Colleen Alles

Chapbooks
  Three Stars
  So What to Say to a Bird
  Porch Light to the Longshoreman
  Induction: Poems for My Daughter

Fiction
  Skinny Vanilla Crisis

Contents

IV. REPLY HAZY, TRY AGAIN.

V. MY SOURCES SAY NO.

VI. As I see it, yes.

OUTLOOK NOT SO GOOD.

Phases

If you thought
the moon was missing
one piece this morning, like
 a bone-white china cup
 carelessly dropped
 by someone,

please remember:
 the moon is always whole—

It's just sometimes
she will show you
 her whole shape,
 her roundness, her grace
when she is reflecting
hot light from the sun.

Other times

she won't.

Lake Michigan

Hold out your hands
  and let me give you every
  long look
  deep sigh
  and daydream
  I've had for years now.

And when you laugh
  because your palms are still
    empty,

   go see the smooth
    beach stones
    gathered
  on the shoreline.

Please remember
  that beach stones
    have round edges
  because the waves and the wind
    kept handling
      them, kept pushing them
  over and over
against the sand.

Those rocks are polished
  for how far
    they have traveled
  from where they began.

    You might think
a long journey
  or constant
    abrasion with sand
      might make any stone rough.
   No.
The wind and the waves and the sand
  and time

and the long travels
only soften.
Only soften.
Only leave smoothness
behind.
Only leave behind a gentleness
in their wake

I find precious.

Hold out your hand
and let me leave you
with a smooth stone
from this shoreline,
and when you hold it,
please think of me and
remember that
I understand

Lake Michigan. I understand
her waves and the wind that pushes
her stones to shore. I know of the scores
of rocks

she hides below her surface.

Think of the waves and the wind and
of me
when you hold that
worn-down rock
and know that I

had such a hard time
putting you
down, too.

Skirmish

Since the door slam,
my fingers have stroked
the beaded cord of the chain
lamp in the hallway half
a dozen times. Soon, I expect
I will pull. Soon, I expect I will

settle for a seat
in the darkness, wait for you
to return quietly, slowly,
perhaps not

expecting my pale face to open
like a barred owl on a bare limb,
static as she listens for the hint

of a mouse skittering
in the underbrush.

A Mercy

It's like when a dream
tells you you're dreaming.

    Let the nightmare dissolve,
    it says.
This is a mirage. Your worst fears
    are works
    of fiction.

And you realize
your dream could have let you
keep on dreaming.
You realize a dream never owed you
    anything.

A dream doesn't have to tell
    you you're dreaming.

Just as
    tonight, you didn't need
    to pick up the phone

even though I kept her
    ringing.

Grief is an item on a menu I don't want

at a restaurant I didn't ask to go to in the first place. But
here we are. We can't leave until I've ordered, & don't
ask how, but I understand this without being told, &
every choice is wrong. Every choice is wrong. We are not
supposed to be here. I shred the napkin in my lap. Then
I shred yours. I spy a straw wrapper by your fork. Time
to rip the thin white paper, & as I do, I remember an old
friend used to tie knots in her straw wrappers. Then, she'd
pull. If the knot was undone in the pulling—if it came
apart in a gentle way, the paper able to let go of the knot
that had been holding it together—then the person she
most admired loved her, too. So then instead of ripping,
I worry the straw wrapper in my fingers until it's worn &
ragged & crinkled—so used up now & frail & delicate
& so overwhelmed by the tidal wave of heartbreak that
when I finally tie a knot and then pull hard on both ends,
it has absolutely no choice but to break in my hands.

You don't know

this, but one time, a few weeks after you called it off,
I saw you at the supermarket. You were hunched over
a sweet onion, running your thumb over its skin. You
didn't see me, holding my breath among the bananas.

Your face looked distant and distracted, maybe even sad.
And when you finally placed the fifth contender in your
black basket, my mind combusted with the question,
What in the world was wrong with any of the others?

You Were Moving

you said.
South.

So to me,
you became

a late
summer
migratory bird.

I almost mentioned then:
when I first learned
of the ruby-throated hummingbird,

nothing
in the world
had ever
so amazed me.

Maybe not the prettiest
bird, but

as you said goodbye,
I thought,

Why can't we all be named
for the part of us we wish

everyone else would see?

Ruby-throated hummingbird,
I am your big-hearted woman.

I am the woman
who has always loved you.

I will let you see me cry
when you finally fly away.

How are you?

I would say it's a bit like a lamp left
on in the other room:
It burns and is no real danger,
        not like the wood-wick candle
           we forgot
      on the mantle the night you
      said my lips addicted you.

So there's only a little light now
coming from the low-watt globe,
and it's getting easier to walk by. It's

      a little bulb still trying,
      an ember casting
      a little shadow there by the rug.

And I have a little feeling
      each time I walk
      barefoot
      down the hall,
      I ought to go

      and turn it off
      since neither of us is
            in the room
            anymore
            at all.

We are aware of the weeds

How the golden

      dandelions

clump   in the side yard
     a dozen   at a time

as if
      someone

      from their past
whispered
      a secret to the seeds.

Congregate
      if you can. Land together,
      if you can. Together

      when you can.

I wish
      on your behalf

the soil soaks you up. That you share

      in the abundance
      of the rain.

      That you take
from the sun what you need.

      That the
earth
will insist

      you
all
grow up   this way.

Autumn Leaves on the Sidewalk

As I pull the hound along
on our evening walk,
I suppose I shouldn't give
the wind all the blame.

After all, if all they needed was
a gentle nudge—the lightest
whisper of invisible touch—

then some leaves are just waiting
for the wind to take them
all the way down

to the ground.

After a Storm

Once in a gridiron downpour, I remembered too late
the dandelion bedsheet on the backyard clothesline,
and that I'd never secured her to the nylon with pins.
And you, the last time you left me on a ball diamond
by third base, I think. It's hard to remember. It's hard
to be aware of more these days than the sweat pooling
in the small of my back, right in the swell you liked
to touch best, the divot where you let your fingertips rest.

There was that look in your eye, a white line in the dirt
leading me on, and the threat of a rain that was coming.
Later, with all my apologies, I picked up that bedsheet
in her heap. Like me, she'd spent the afternoon dancing
in the wind, had dirtied the hem of her dress. I spat at
the elm as I balled her up, heavy against my body. Slick
with mud—it's always such a mess before it's all clean.
I took us home, after the rain. A place I knew we'd be safe.

BETTER NOT TELL YOU NOW.

Voyeurism

In an hour, the kitchen light
in the dove-white house next door will flicker

on, and I'll stand at the window,
my palms around a hot mug of black coffee,

listening for signs my son is awake,
remembering the echo of the rain as it ricochets

off the roof, at the window, in the chimney
on its way down. Hard. Swift. Soft. I want

him to need me, but I want to exist in the silent
envelope of the morning, too. Before it's all called

to begin again. Before I take on all their
heaviness, before I make every outcry

a problem I find a way to solve.
They've only caught me once at the window—

the couple next door. Early risers,
coaxing their shoulders into down parkas, they eyed

me good but kept on, locking the side door
behind them. I wanted to explain my ritual then:

that I have sometimes needed to see
the light on somewhere outside my house, as though

some pirate had ferried back from
an extraordinary adventure, sand filling his shoes,

and I still needed to see the dog-eared map as proof
for myself. In the moments before dawn, the lonely ones—

I have needed the bright light of the kitchen
next door. I have needed that house to be awake.

I have needed the sense that someone else
was listening and remembering the rain beside me.

After a Party

I.

I want silence.
The house wants silence,
the floorboards are exhausted,

but don't you feel that heartache in the walls
by the kitchen
        where we gathered for hours,
        elbows and bodies and shoulders touching,
        drinks sloshing,
music notes lilting the conversation
till someone invented the idea to dance?

II.

The party is chaos
        that sprang from nothing.

The party is a firework
        of joy and sound and light,
        an energy we planned but cannot understand.

And we are drawn to each other,
we gather together,
round mountains crowding a fire because

        who knows when it all will end
        and in shadows and sudden silence,
we will only watch the last sparks of light
love leaves to trace the dark night sky.

III.

Which is why,
I think,
when I joined you in the kitchen
for another drink,

you began to tell
the story of that time
we kissed

and the power went out—
        not even for a snow storm
        or an ice storm or a wind storm.
We were not,
as they say
in the Midwest,
"having weather,"

we were having coffee.
We were new.
We were nervous.
We were inventing the idea to dance.

That kiss was a firework
        of joy and sound and light
        and you were looking at me
        and my heart was chaos that sprang from nothing
        an energy I could not understand

as you leaned in to kiss me and then

First Date in a Bookstore

What you can't hear
when you open
the cover, cradle the spine
in your palm,
and place your finger
on the first cream page

is the sigh from
the opening sentence,
its voice as it whispers,

Thank you,
it's been so long
since I've been
touched.

Sleeping dogs lie

He owns nothing in the world
but a signature
way of sleeping:

His back pressed against my leg,
his head resting on my knee.

I imagine he dreams of
a rabbit.

Why not? He almost caught one
last night,
chasing the hare from the garden,

his salmon tongue
lobbing hard
when he finally returned.

I asked how close he came
to the heels,

studying his soft eyes for
answers. He did

not answer.
But who knows. Maybe he's not
chasing anything at all,
right now as he's sleeping,

and he'd laugh
if he ever knew I
speculate

on his dreams—
the ones that twitch his paws,
elicit low whimpers. Like me,

perhaps he has a litany
of secrets he would never admit to,
even while asleep. He is sometimes

with the world in a way
I can't be, understands things

I think. He is sometimes like me.
In a way.

He is, maybe, not chasing
but wrestling
the world. His world.
Everything he understands.

Like me, perhaps
he has
his own ghosts to unwrap
in the darkness.

Winter Solstice

When you sent me
      for a long walk this afternoon
little did you know how
the bare branches by the river

would get me dreaming, that I'd miss
      your voice calling me in for tea.

By the tall reeds near the shoreline
      I nearly fell in love with the brightest

part of the day. They tell me

the days that remain get longer from here,
      stretching to the middle of June,

      that all the greatest days get better
from here, arching out till forever.

      I bet I can keep on this path

by the wild bushes, let the branches
      touch me when I'm listless,
      listen for your voice on the wind,
      promise everyone

the reeds will always thrush in restlessness.
      But I keep returning after every walk,

      a crumbling leaf between my fingers,
      a new tale to tell you about its

falling.

Seven Reasons This House is a Woman

1. I feel it the most by the fireplace because the pilot light is her heart, ready at any moment to become a flame.

2. Once, when you and I were in the middle of a barn burner, a pan fell suddenly off its rack in the kitchen, and that clamor told us to calm the hell down. Everything was actually fine.

3. I recovered the original floor plans from the city archives. She was meant to have a laundry chute, built-in bookshelves, a big closet near the sink. Someone had changed her mind.

4. This house breathes. This house sighs. This house tucks me in each night.

5. This house forgives our daughter for picking loose entryway tiles with her idle, nimble fingers.

6. Her side stoop invites me to sit down at the end of a humid summer day. She says, have a beer with me. Stretch out those legs. I do not mind the circle of sweat your bottle will leave on my cement.

7. Last summer, I found a thick chunk of plaster in the yard. I turned the piece over in my palm, examining the layers of exterior paint. I saw her in a new way when I saw how well she had learned to keep secrets.

Daydream

It was the song on the radio, you say. It was the light
hangover you still feel from last night that lays

not unpleasantly on your mind, turning it over
on this road, letting your thoughts wander

from the curve of my cheek, my lips,
my thigh, and the bends of this road.

You were staring at the birds gathering in roadside
trees and without realizing, you were looking for

my favorite, my songbird. Or you were looking for
any clue that the brightest among them

would suddenly send out a silent call, rally her troops,
begin to take flight without you.

Possible Scene of an Accident

Forgive me for drinking
all the coffee today.

I didn't start a second pot
before I set out for the morning
as though at the urging of some great
wilderness explorer
who raised his hat, winked at me, and
with a coal-black voice said go.

Who knows what will happen today.

Not the farmhouse on the corner,
not the roads glistening still with rain.

Who knows what will happen at this intersection
where this street greets the next.

Maybe you can tell me tonight,
when I finally
make my way home
it'll be dark again.
I'll hope to find you wiping your mug
clean from the kitchen sink,
then mine,
then the restlessness
from my eyes leftover
from this morning.

May-December Romance

the sky watches me
stand   underneath

    everyone watches me
stand   underneath
really,

in awe of all your snowflakes,
hoping I   am
really   frozen,

    waiting to see if you'll stick.

Marriage

First, find a level place on the Earth.

Remove the trees, even though it feels like a shame.

Ensure this is a flat place,
a solid, certain area.

In fact, this might be the most important step.
Don't skip this one.

If you hurry too fast to find the right
well-squared piece of land, the
remaining steps won't matter.

You will want
to take your time
with the cornerstone.

You will need
the heaviest brick
in your corner.

I'm no architect,
but the rest is
all artistry and physics,
a polite and ginger defiance of gravity.
The construction of a building
puffing out its chest with steel trusses
so it won't someday
cave in on itself.

After some time, the roof will follow, and then, other people
may enter.

For now, wonder at the vertical slats, the piles of plywood,
the perfect shadows all this casts on the ground
you chose.

The River Liffey

I went to the River Liffey to leave it all behind—some pain for the waves, a pinch of salt off the block of my body. I thought they would crumble off easy—those parts of me I no longer wanted. Leave them at the River Liffey, I thought. Some think it means *life*. A woman walked by, carrying a baby. Next, a man with a felt hat, dressed in an overcoat that had seen kinder weather. Neither looked my way. The River Liffey flows through the center of the city, its mouth to Dublin Bay. No one tells you how to grieve the part of yourself you most want to bury under the deepest water, give over to the coldest wave. No one teaches you how to look like you fit in when you don't feel like everyone else, when you don't feel like *anyone* else, for that matter. Nor how to be at home in your own body, how to be at home in your own body anywhere in the world. The River Liffey leaves her tributaries, continues on to the Irish Sea. I'm not the first to stand on her banks, ramble my thoughts as tourists, locals pass by. A young girl in bright pink galoshes, holding her father's pinkie. Next, a man with black hair, a paperback under his arm. He smiled at me. Finally I stood, brushed off at the knees. I made the River Liffey a graveyard for the parts of me I no longer wanted. She was once named something else, I read. She was once named *for* something else. *An Ruirthech*. It means *fast runner*, I read. Maybe a woman who runs faster for shedding the parts it's time to leave behind. *Strong* runner. Maybe a river that runs stronger for every part she can leave behind.

YOU MAY RELY ON IT.

Birds by the Attic Slats

Brown songbirds have pressed themselves through the attic slats
       by the roof of the house next door. To enter, they
       pull their wings against their little bodies,
       slipping inside
       the attic to brace for
       the coming colder months.

My son and I watch from the window
       as the birds come and go.
We point with our fingers. We touch the cold glass pane,
       offering to the birds our fingertips.

On occasion, my son rests his head on my chest
       as he did the week he was born.
The curls of his crown
       become down and feathers
       under my lips.
He pulls his tiny bones
       into his round body,
       pressing against my exterior
       like he wants to pull himself through
       my walls—
       like he wants
       to access an attic
       I am not aware I have:
a place
that is warm
       and safe
       and quiet
       and ready for the coming winter
and it's inside of me.

He rests his head against me the way I have learned we all
        should when we have chanced upon
        a good place to
        seek warmth and safety.

And this is the way I have learned we are all
meant to rest against one another

when we have found
        another human to love,
        if only for just one season.

The News of the World

Death is nothing at all.
It does not count.
I have only slipped away into the next room.
Nothing has happened.
Everything remains exactly as it was.
−Henry Scott Holland

The news of the world will all be bad this morning,
so let's not listen. Let's press our hands instead on
cool lined paper, sink back into lavender sheets. A
deep sigh will do, too, and you drift back to sleep
with all your worries tucking themselves back
into the wrinkles around your brown eyes.

It's an odd life—well, perfectly ordinary—but strange
to craft a raft of our own without knowing how long
we'll all float here together, happy—happy, though
the rest of the world seems to be a sea of discontent.
Content, though of course it is the way of the sea
to call us each away in turn to depths beyond our reach.

Once, I read an author write that death is someone
you love only living in the next room of the house.
They have not left; they are still there. Maybe you
catch footsteps from time to time, hear the sound
of their laughter over the coffee grinder, the hum
of the water splattering in the kitchen sink.

This is news for another morning, and these are words
of worry for another time, meant for me to read back
later. Later, like waves hitting the shore. Today when
you wake, we'll warm you with our bodies in turn,
coax you from dreams to daylight, and when you open
your hands for that first cup of coffee it will bring you

34   to life.

As we wind down

Thank you for saying
this year is only a metaphor
for a true story, like something you

once heard at a bar—a joke a man
told a woman in a back corner booth,
just to make her laugh. Sometimes we sit

on the back porch—you and me—
despite December, passing
between us mulled wine, back

and forth, as though we think
we can hide from the whole world behind
our little house, and tell the stack

of these months they can't reach us here—
like we think this is a place where solitude
is a hymn whose words we sing

on Sundays, and I am not pressed
to conceal the places on my body
where the seams have worn the hardest,

where you tell me even if I am threadbare,
it's okay. The world may see it anyway,
but who cares? The wisemen would've wished

for wine if they'd thought to. The wisemen
did not have you. Thank you for you, for warm
wine, for your hand reaching out to mine, for

our porch in late December. Christmas morning's
a stone's throw away, and what is a miracle,
I think, except when the world gives you

exactly what you want in a way so different
than how you asked for it, but yet—
and yet. It's okay. The world may see

it anyway, but who cares? Even if I am threadbare.
Thank you for you. You're a miracle. This year is
a disaster. It's a wonder just the same.

If you are alone
for Galway Kinnell, for "Wait", with thanks

You are not alone.

You are still two
feet on the pavement,
two arms at your sides,

and if you're not that, then

you're still ten thousand days—
twenty thousand days.
Are you not

the sum of each day,

or
not even the sum—

are you not
a litany of days in a particular order,
organizing themselves
like a parade

inside you
so that you do not
have to feel

alone
when you are alone.

If you are alone,
there is still your reflection

in a shop's
glass mirror, even if
you refuse to see it

head to toe,
it will show you whatever
your body is to you now, and whatever
your body is to you
now is

still the sum of your life, yet

not even the sum. The parade.

Do not forget to watch the parade.

I hope you watch it. I hope you feel it.
I hope you do not feel alone

because you are not alone,
even if you find yourself
by yourself

as you glance in that shop
window,

as you lead the beautiful
parade inside your body
of twenty thousand days, or as you

sit for a few moments
with your own
history,

exactly
as you are
today.

Let your history
reassure you

you are beautiful,
you are loved. You are

worth everything,
worth every single thing.

You are not alone.
You are quite simply

the most wonderful
most wonderful most wonderful
parade.

Horoscope

Today you will strike
a fight with your own bones
for a pretty petty reason.
It's not unfamiliar, perhaps,
to be at such odds
with the most foundational
parts of yourself, but
nonetheless, you'll act
as though it's the first time
anyone's ever been at sixes &
sevens with their own insides.
Your heart may join in; let her.
She's stronger after every fight
and also, hasn't yet forgiven you
a few things.

You know what.

Eventually, everything will come
back together for you, and it will
feel a little like when you spy
two strangers across a room—
a nearly empty room—and as
they slowly advance toward
one another, you are filled
with fascination bordering on
obsession at the sudden thought—
the sudden realization—
when they finally meet &
gently shake hands that by God,
they knew each other
all along.

January, 11 Degrees

I.

I've never loved you more than when
you ran down the middle of the road
at midnight, fat snowflakes in your
black hair, cursing the name of the last man
to leave me with a heartache the size of

Lake Superior.

II.

Later tonight and quite impossibly, I'll
leave my parka in the basement of J.
Gardella's Tavern where we'll karaoke 90s
love songs from bands with boys whose
faces used to cover our

wide-ruled notebooks.

III.

I should be cold, but I don't feel anything
at all. Then I wake up on your futon and it's
morning and I'm warm, we get my coat back
and look, you've done it again: You've made me
know no hurt, no man, no one will ever freeze me

over completely.

Reveal

You, like me,
dared to mingle
a couple blushing wishes
in with silent prayer—

so maybe now
we make it up to the Father,
Son, and Holy Ghost
at vespers in the evening.

From my back pocket
I pull three rosy plumbs
of pitcher's thistle, prickly
postcards from the dunes

whose curves and arcs
we climbed all morning. Here
by the water, I'm just
so thankful for everything.

Push aside the lily pads, give
your palms to the weeds. Welcome
the pond scum gumming
by your fingers. Never

mind the mess: an offering is
an offering. Sometimes when we reach
inside ourselves, a remnant from
the shoreline is all we have

for the giving.

In the doorframe

Lean your body back
       like you're up against
       the willow in the yard

       where you were raised—

the one that shed a hundred
limbs & branches.

At least I do. Another tree
in another
state might await
       you in your memory.

Or maybe
it's a beach—a shoreline in any season,
       a deep lake so beautiful

you squint because she's too much
to take in all at once.

Dig your shoulder blades
around the edges. Take a breath. It feels nice.

If you can,
       touch the other side.

It's usually then
       I pretend

the previews are over, the movie's
about to start, & I can't believe who it is
       I'm sitting with in the dark.

It brings
me comfort, is all I mean—I am happy
& I am hopeful, & I am
lost
in a good memory.

Insomuch
as it's a word
we use too much

      this is
      joy
      in the doorframe.

If a house could
wrap its arms
      around you, it would.
When a house
finds you standing
      between two
      rooms for hours,
      & more than

once in the middle of the night,
      it knows.

You might be years from
where you started, & miles from
      those you love the most.

Still. A house can do its best
to hold you, just
      do its best by you,
      every day,
      bringing you comfort

the only way that it can.

To my son, who falls asleep at night with the light on

I heard it said once
that the planets are on

a *march* around the sun.

> In that moment
> it occurred to me
> I was taught it only
as *revolution*. Which is

a beautiful word for the journey,
> don't get me wrong.

But *march* speaks
> to the work
> at hand, the truth
> of every step

one after the other. Continuous.
> Without failure. March
> reminds me of the part
> where none of the planets ever

give up. Everyone stays steady.
Everyone keeps moving. March
> is measured and without
> change. Don't you think?
> Consider

all the planets marching. Consider
all the planets
> allowed to carry on
> their own path
> at a deliberate pace
> of their own making,

and every other planet
is content to let it be so,

and the sun watches from the middle,
rejoicing.

We need to talk about tadpoles

for Mara

We need to talk
about when

to live at all
means
you must become
so different from your past—

When
to be alive
is to travel
an invisible trajectory

until you are so foreign
to yourself,

until you feel like a tourist in
the place you were born—

And then
we'll need to talk about
if it's better to know

when you're in between

about the grand thing
you are
destined to become—

about all
the big and beautiful things
that've been planned
for you
all along?

Anniversary

I know: Let's walk by your old apartment—
the one above that bar, the one where we
slept on a mattress on the floor & I killed
all your houseplants. Let's stop in for a drink.
Let's pass the parking meter I collided with
once—the one that knocked the wind out of me.
You laughed, but only once I said I was all right.
I used to fall asleep every night with my head
on your chest. We used to share a full size
bed. We won't get carded, that's for sure.
We can talk about the hairless cat, that big
bath tub. How your skin felt like fresh sheets.
The shouts of the drunks leaving the bar at
two in the morning, & how we knew we
were old when they began to feel annoying.
We moved not long after that. I would like
to apologize again for the plants. I confess
I do miss that cat, that apartment, & that bed.
We can sit at the bar & look out the window
onto Commerce street. I know: Maybe we'll see
a man with a wide smile, & a woman wearing
strappy shoes that appear to hurt her feet. They'll
be awake far later than us tonight. We will go home,
pay the sitter, check on the kids, lock the back door.
Maybe I will think of them at two a.m.—the couple,
I mean, when I wake from an odd dream about
nothing (or to visit the bathroom yet again). Two
a.m.: closing time. Maybe if I listen, I will hear
them leaving the bar, the woman in bare feet on the street,
the man holding her close, & I'll roll over in our bed,
find a new place on your chest to rest my head, & smile.

REPLY HAZY, TRY AGAIN.

Haunted

Are we to agree
a ghost is

any shadow caught
on the wall that can't
be blamed

on light from the lamp,

or the large bay window
in the living room?

Does ghost mean
any moment

I am in the kitchen
slicing apples
with a paring knife,
edging the sharp blade
to my palm but never

drawing blood? Is it

when my dog
stares east
past the bramblebush
in gray December

for
so long
at nothing,

or how my children,
when I hold them,

both pat my shoulder
the way my grandmother
once did? To which I add

the memory of the man
in the tire store
who struck a profile
so much like the man
I used to really love

my heart waited
a long moment to even
beat in its cage again,

so certain
of its history

it could only widen
its gaze,
hold its breath,

absolutely suspended.

Petoskey Stones

The hickories thicken near the fork in the creek
where we're just out of sight of our mother.
The last time we were here, in late August, you threw
a slew of dirty pennies in the dark water and made me
swear to keep secret forever the name of your
most serious crush.

Which I already knew. I read your diary. You
compared his eyes to Petoskey stones—the ones
Mom found at that tourist shop in the U.P. the week
we spent there, sharing a bed. You rubbed coconut
sunscreen on your stomach between your bikini pieces
each morning.

She surprised us on that trip—Mom did—taking pleasure
in teasing us, I think. She'd bought the smooth souvenirs
when we weren't looking, hiding her hands behind her
back till we tickled them out of her, one at a time.

Later, when you went back to the hotel pool to see
if that cute boy was still there, I held my rock as Mom
hung my one-piece to dry on the high steel shower rod,
and I felt the weight

of the words she told me coming back from the bathroom
—that everything between me and you would soon change—

dropping like heavy stones in the water.

Elegy for a Pigeon

But mostly, I think back to the spring I was 16 and introduced
myself for the first time to New York City. The epic climb

to the top of the Empire State Building burned my thighs,
but I chose to save the exposures in my disposable camera for

the teal and charcoal pigeons that cooed and jutted their necks
my way in a campaign to learn if I had carried with me any crumbs.

I felt I understood those pigeons better than all the other two-bit
tourists who elbowed me from the viewfinders on the Observation

Deck, ready to take their turn at surveying the lovely harbor. Back home,
I was in love with a boy I was sure didn't know my name. For hours,

I would stare at the back of his neck in U.S. History class. For a quarter,
that morning, I had bought that boy a postcard of our Lady Liberty

and immediately tucked it inside the front cover of my diary. I'd never
mail it—that was a given. Mailing a postcard to a boy who doesn't love

you is like a pigeon sitting on a pier, fancying himself a swan. I think
if bird breeds were chess pieces, a pigeon would be asked to be a pawn.

We'd entrust them to helmet up and prepare for battle. We'd call
for their sacrifice for the fact of their obvious abundance. We'd judge

them ineffectual, only able to advance one space at a time. We'd lose
sight of them, think that just because they are ordinary they are not

important. We would regard them as expendable. Like everyone. Like
anyone. Like I am just any girl sitting behind you, studying your skin. But I

believe I am one of a kind. I believe I am not someone you should take
for granted. What is the right way to write a pigeon the kind of elegy

it deserves? A common bird resplendent in his abundance. In the end,
I'm really asking a pigeon to tell me the secret of how I could be Queen.

Mourning, although I must say

This would be a better poem
if I were handy
with a metaphor, or
if I could lay
on your mind

an artful image, like the stone
birdbath in the yard next door,
overgrown
with moss and ivy.

That's a simile, though—
a way to say something gently,
I've always thought.
A way to ease
into something.

I'd still love to find
the best way
to share this morning
with you,

as right before six,
I stepped outside
with a cup of black coffee.
I drew in a lungful
of early April air and there
in the east

hung the moon,
incredibly bright and
  so low
  so big
  so heavy

she seemed to weigh
the whole world
without actually trying.

Take a gander

This is where I met you. But really, it's all right
    if you don't remember a spot by a staircase.

After all, that place wouldn't really mean anything
    if it wasn't where I first saw your face. Although—

& as you know—I didn't love you until later. Years later.
    But now, I can't walk by that spot without the echo

of your voice rampaging in my imagination. I would bet
    that patch of carpet never thought it would be

of particular note. Significance is not something to which
    I imagine carpet aspires. It only wants to cover floor

boards, right? It only tries to fulfill the mission imparted
    at its origins. It only has a job it wants to do. So did

I, I suppose, although I do understand now that nothing
    ever plans to form bonds & attachments this heavy

& thick to the soul of another person, just as I see now no
    place regards itself as special up until the moment

that finally, it becomes.

The poem in which I pretend

I don't care about you at all, & so certainly,
I am not going to pick up the phone, break down & ask after
how you are, how you are, how you are.

How are you? Did you beat the heat this afternoon, or did you let her
hang her wet heavy arms on your shoulders? Are you a little
like the edges of the red crumbled bricks on Wealthy Street

near the hot dog joint, the one I ran by this morning just after dawn,
sweating & sweating, running & running, & thinking of you,
& the only soul who paid me any mind was the blue-eyed husky

fenced in the front yard of the house on the corner at Norwood Southeast?
He eyed me like I'm a woman who isn't sure of the world, of where
she belongs, of where she will call home tonight. He eyed me like

I'm a woman who isn't exactly sure to where she is running.

Downed limbs

& sometimes they
laugh, & okay—that's all

right, & all right, too,
when you stop & stand alone

next to them
after a thunderstorm—

in the weeds, by the waves,
down the dock this afternoon.

There is
everywhere is

every other thing also
misunderstood. Here is

a silo of words unsaid.
Its shadow in the grass.
Tall as you've ever seen.
Some courage, I think.
I think. Praise be

the willow tree
who never let anyone

stop her.

Finding a rifle under the bed

I.

On some beaches, the sand lies
clean and tan and warm, a veritable carpet
for those relentless waves.

But water chops away at whatever
land answers the call to border it.

There is not always a smooth
line between earth and water.

II.

You stand a few feet back from the
shoreline with your gun

and I stand a few feet back from you,
the loud pop of the trigger,
the white clouds from your cigarette.

when it hits me

III.

you will always be a faceless mystery,
water and earth and smoke to me.

We use skin

The body keeps
a record of everything.

When I look at my son,
I see the scar
on his lip from where he fell

one morning before dawn.
I worried he wouldn't stop crying.

Maybe he will never
notice the scar

that twists his smile—
a permanent record.

A permanent record
that twists his smile:
notice the scar.

Maybe he will never.

I worried he wouldn't stop crying
one morning before dawn.

On his lip from where he fell,
I see the scar.

When I look at my son:
a record of everything
the body keeps.

Holding close a breeze

Maybe
you can
teach me
how
to be
a lighter
version
of myself.

Not so
heavy.
Not so
over-
whelmed
by
everything.

I'm over-
whelmed
by like
every
single
thing.

Can you
please
teach me,

like how
I imagine—

I mean,
don't you
just
picture

a tornado
holding close
a breeze,

from
time
to
time,

whispering
in her ear,

All you are
really
meant to do
is lightly
touch
this
world
all around

you.

Flourish

I've been with the sugar maple all afternoon, the one
who laid her roots by the river like there was no way

she would allow a shallow embankment or the constant
threat of oncoming waves to shy her away. I told her

about the mountains I've been climbing lately—the ones
who disguise themselves as hills. They aren't. I let her

scarlet canopy calm me to the bone. Do you have all
afternoon, I asked, and before I'm back home telling

everyone I touched your smooth bark to my skin for a time,
I'd like to lay my head down, maybe leave the mountains

at your feet if you let me. Let's talk about the trees who never
dare the shoreline. What if I'm bound for the orchard?

What if I never find the strength, if I never get brave?
Honey, I imagine she'd say. You'll do just fine. Take

a rest from all your climbing. You'll land where you
are meant to land and dig your roots in deep. Nothing

stops a seed that's chosen where it's going. Never mind
some pain. A wave is just some water till it's breaking.

MY SOURCES SAY NO.

Love Poem #55

Yes.

That was me who found
a pair of speckled fawns
late in returning home, and then

an excuse to walk down your street
last night,

kicking the thistle, shushing
the hermit thrushes, and dammit

if the milkweed didn't
tell me to go home,
too.

Compline[1] for January 1st

At the sight of the fir tree laid bare
on her side, inches from the curb,
I let my breath out slow. Of course

I know it's time to store the ornaments,
the nativity scene, to take outside
this beautiful, living thing we asked

to stand among us for weeks like family.
At each day's close, we turned off her bright
lights, whispered our private goodnights.

I could not shutter the house to that tree
without touching those soft branches one
final time. I needed to say that I'm sorry.

I'd say out loud—if she had ears with which
to listen—there's never a good time to let go
of something that's been so important;

if I thought she'd take my words to heart,
I'd say to her there's never a good time
to let go of something that's been so beautiful.

---

1 **compline** / ˈkämplin / *noun*
a service of evening prayers forming part of the Divine Office of the Western
Christian Church, traditionally said (or chanted) before retiring for the night
(Oxford Languages).

May 25, 2020

Today   my kids tried to pick   pink
flowers growing in
our neighbor's   yard,

and I said no,
stop it
stop it.

And they didn't understand
because the other   day we were

a rush to grab   all the yellow dandelions
growing in   the outlawn,

and now,   my voice was shaking
as I shooed

my son, my daughter

back to our yard,

saying   let's go home   and
I'm sorry   and

I never   should have told you
one flower   was worth
anything more
than any other.

Every few days

that blue jay returns
        to my feeder

        to see if I've
offered the seeds he is
seeking.

With a thrash of his tail, he flies
        away, to a neighbor

who can offer him more.

        He isn't
(God bless him)
        afraid to show me:
he'd rather be off
        to another place,

someone who can give him
what he's needing.

Poem of Parting

I.

So you held a bird.

You saw her silhouette
descend from the elm—impossible.
The feathers were a marvel,
the lightness of her body on yours.

II.

So what to say to a bird?

It won't be long that you stay.
Any small movement will scare you away.
Please know I'll keep the tracks of your feet
on my palms long after you've flown away.

From a Seedling

In my backyard, a sapling
        grows where an old tree once lived,

and if I were better at identification,
        I would tell what kind: maple, or elm.

I don't know. For some reason, I never
        took interest in discerning

one type of tree from another.
        I never too much cared.

But I also was not one
        to shy away from rough bark.

I can't say how many times
        my fingertips have given

tacit praise to all the trees
        that will outlive me,

or how fervently I apologized
        to the tree I agreed to see

cut down. Yes, it was time.
        Yes, it was dead.

Still. I held
        its thick trunk in my palms

the night before
        men came with chainsaws

just to say
        I am in awe of the long life

you lived so close to me.

Root Systems

Give me your coldest winter
and I will close it in my fist,
press it
with the weight of my red fingers

and tell you, No.

The worst winter wasn't the one
the weatherman warned us about.

It wasn't the one
whose relentless snowdrifts
finally caved the curved eaves of our roof,

and broke one by one
all the branches
of the centenarian trees
that stood as sentries
by the mailbox. They told

anyone who came to our door
Listen.
There is peace and beauty here.
Walk this soft path and
Listen. Here,
there is finally love and home.

No.

The most unforgiving winter
was the one that
caved the eaves of my insides,
broke the branches protecting my heart, and
took the new life you and I had just made

for itself.

Three Words for Sunset

In an effort
     to slip back

under the dark wave of dreams at 3 a.m., I think

     of a sunset:
bright; red; glowing. How else could I
describe it but
     slow, warm, inevitable.

Under the quilt, my wrist

brushes your back, my knuckles find the crags
of your spine.
     Gentle—I don't mean

to wake you, exactly; I'd like to fall back
asleep. Love to, really. Or, I'd love
     to tell you a story:

for the better part
of this afternoon, our son
was inconsolable. A lost marble—truly. Yes.

     That was the thing. A tiny glass orb won
     with a quarter from some supermarket machine.

My dress was a handkerchief, his pink
face wrinkled

with grief. I picked him up, pulled him tight
     to the crescent
     of my hip, let his hot breath

hit my neck.

The blue marble may have disappeared
        forever, I don't tell him.

        It's around here somewhere, I tell him.
It'll return on its own terms.

I don't know how to say
        maybe we never find it.
Maybe it never comes back

        and maybe—well, not even maybe,

        definitely, this is just
        the first thing you'll lose—or,

        not even, actually. It's not even the first thing
        you have ever lost.

This might be the first thing you remember losing,
        if it never returns

on its own terms. I don't know.
        I don't know

        if I have the words,
I just

let him rest his forehead on my collarbone
        till I heard

        a sigh come from deep in his body,
till he let his arms go limp

against me. Big sigh. Big sigh. There, there.
It's okay.
        It's going to be okay.

Give me

three words for loss: Bright, red, glowing.

Three more:
      slow, warm,
            inevitable.

Counsel

The cardinal I spotted between two maples has
a look about him I would like to take home.

He knows how to marshal the wind whenever
he decides to arise. He knows the secret, I think,
of taking a tough force of nature and coaxing it
until it's a friend.

From the ground, the red bird cocks his head, juts his sharp
beak my way. I have made a sound, I guess, or perhaps
the old hound has beside me.

I see now there's no trace of the snow that came on
so suddenly this morning, when—well into April—we were
not expecting winter to spit out one last spasm,
like she just couldn't let us go without taking one more swing
at her favorite season.

And so I resolve to say the hard things tonight,
uncertain as we head for the house how long that cardinal
will stay. I am aware—I am only thinking as the wind picks up:

I am only really certain of my steps on the hard ground
in the field at twilight, the *pad pad pad* of my best friend
matching my stride, his tail a metronome as I ask him home,

the red bird a postcard from another country very far away
that by magic has somehow made its way to me.

Summer as a map

"I thought I could describe a state; make a map of sorrow."
—C. S. Lewis, *A Grief Observed*

In June, it was the peonies
at the side stoop,
    heavy with bloom
and folding over each other, offering
    a model
for how to share comfort
in grief.

One afternoon I took a book
to the park and ignored
it for hours
    to stare at couples holding hands;
    at midnight I realized
I'd left it spine-up
    near some hydrangeas.

July brought with her
fireflies glowing at twilight.
    I don't tell my daughter
the lighting up part is just
a show put on to attract a mate.

Then the fog lay over the lake
one morning, so thick from a distance
    it asked to be spooled
like wool, brought home
as mist on a spindle.

And in August:
a family of Canada geese
ambled through the beach grass,

craned their slender necks
in unison.   I watched the six of them
without breathing,

saw their black
throats become question marks
before me.   Imagined their tongues
ready to hiss, resting in beaks,
        aware of the threat I posed;
        they were willing to take flight
        if need be,

but first, they would bid me
not
        to come closer.

neighbors

I am pretty certain I just ran by
your new house, your new dog
your new wife. Your mailbox
looks nice. Do you ever get a
postcard from your old life?

As I see it, yes.

Till August

If you ask the red swing dress hanging
in my closet, she can tell you what it's like
to be a watermelon in July: full and round

and—if you're really ready to level with me—
quite ripe as well. In Michigan, the seasons
don't always choose to follow the rules.

The gutsiest robins ignore their bedtimes, too.
Sometimes, I wear heels that rub raw my red toes
and render me barefoot in the street by your house—

which is how I know your sidewalk spiked a fever
last night, and what makes me want to ask you now:
Did you already know a summer night can arch

your whole life's curve so sweetly? Or is that a truth
I will teach you in the weeks to come as you search
for the last black seeds in your bedsheets till August?

Checking on the baby

for Lincoln

Do not mind, please,
the whisper of my finger-

tips on your skin after dark.
I am only answering

the call every mother
has heard to read your spine

like dots of Braille, to ask
your back to arch in sleep

so that even while you dream,
you will find a way

to echo every letter
of your life to me.

Sonnet for 2020

Never mind—
she just said she doesn't have the energy
to conform to a rhyme scheme.

Don't tell her what
to be about, either. She hasn't

hugged her father in nearly
a year, & it shows, & so she

aches in ways she won't say
except in the pages of her diary.

But she asks you not to worry.
Like a good sonnet, she'll try still
to make order from chaos, leave you
with the impression of

Love.

She remembers
she is lucky to hold
close a heart—& to have stolen time
in a time of so much extra time. Now,
there's laundry to fold, a hound who
begs with his eyes. Someone's made paper
airplanes, a mess on the kitchen floor,
stolen gingerbread from the cookie jar.
That's the stove. Pretty soon,
naptime, bath time, quiet time—

time for a walk at twilight
with the hound, & later,
forgetting she ever tried to be

something she isn't,
there's time
for this sonnet to have a rich,
full glass of sweet red wine.

Hope

I.

I've come to know
Midnight—

her quick style, her
smirk as she says

hey,
you ought to be asleep,

but here you are,
like some

waggish vagabond stirring
creamer into coffee
at an all-night diner.

II.

She says
I get it. You want everyone
to know

you aren't scared
to stare wide open
at the changing of the guard.

III.

She told me

once I saw
a man
at a Craps table

give his fist
a rowdy shake and say
The dice
have no memory,
and thank God for that
as he let the twin cubes
fly
from his fingers.

IV.

It's like that, I think—

tomorrow, I mean.

What comes next.
What comes after.

V.

She says
Yes,
it goes
something like that.

Where to Start

is a good question.

I have found
a person, place, or thing
can make a fine place to start.

Although a time, perhaps, is better.
A thought, or suspicion.
A feeling?

If it is too abstract, then
try something concrete:

a cold pint on a long table
at our first dinner together.

A clear cylinder purposed as a vase,
filled with wine-stained corks.

That waiter who really
rushed our meal—
in my opinion—

or maybe I was just
too uncertain of
where to start
with you.

Let's try these:
        an impression of the third coast in my mind.
        Our hotel key outlining its edges in my pocket.

Or that beautiful woman who
bumped my chair,
spilled my drink,
and touched my arm
upon leaving.

Atlantic

for Micah

When we finally reached the Atlantic after
driving for two days, it was close to midnight.
We ripped off our shoes and socks to walk
the beach, daring the jellyfish to sting our toes.
As the dark Georgia water reflected the moon,
I thought back to the first time I met this ocean.

I was twenty. I was an idiot. I'd been unprepared then,
without a bathing suit or any sense. I'd stripped
down to undergarments and brazenness. I'd waded in,
inviting the cold waves to swell to my pale neck.
Mouthfuls of seawater flooded the parts and pieces
of me I felt were so broken at the time.

I see now my body was always in fine working order.
There were huge ocean liners and impossible fish,
maybe a thousand ancient histories swimming
with me off the coast of Ireland. That day, I wanted
to bottle that feeling. I wished to take the echoes of my
lineage home with me—to sustain me in the years to come.

I wanted to read a paper trail of my ancestors in the waves,
as though the Atlantic could be a full history inked onto
the onion-skin pages of the Old Testament in my family
Bible. I sensed then, at twenty, what I know for sure now.
To take that feeling of understanding home with me
meant I could reach for it, ask it to wash over me at 4 a.m.

when the hard questions life likes to ask knock the loudest
at the door, when I want nothing else but to feel like
that midnight in Savannah with the moon and my
friend's familiar laughter, my fingers safely wrapped
in the hand of the man I'd tried to conjure from the mysteries
of the sea, but had to date only ever formed illusions.

Mid-March in the Midwest

There's the spring breeze
      wresting my door
      from its frame,

      telling everyone
it's high time
      we fall
            in love again.

Where it urges me

in the late afternoon,
      is the shoreline.

      We race and return,
line our pockets
with pebbles. We wrestle

them in the waves, our
fingertips ice, those
      little imitations of rocks
      innumerable.

Who cares
how many there are,

      we find a spot
      for all the stones
still,
line them up at home
      like tin soldiers in the
sill,
the window
      that faces west.

I count the silhouettes
in the dark
     after we kiss goodnight.

Out loud for the evening air

I whisper the perimeters,
     say thank you
     as we
     settle down, settle in,
     say *sleep tight*, and

Now, we get on
     to the dreaming.

Here's something

that feels like a secret
I shouldn't tell:
You are a city I have been to
a lot, lately, and lately I have
spent hours on the sidewalks
of your heart. Sound odd? I have
admired the best face you present
in clean storefront windows, stiff
mannequins on display. It's nice,
of course, all your finery, your face.
But I think you're hiding a universe
under that facade, and I think why
visit a city and only see what any
wanderer can scratch onto a postcard.
Here it is: What I really want,
really, is to know you. I want
to see you underneath. I want to
catch you in the windows
taking down the fake ladies
and the SALE signs. In other words,
I want to see you making way
for something totally new.

The Collective Noun for Octopus is Tangle

An octopus has three hearts, my daughter
says. *Aha*, I say. That sounds like trivia

I've heard before—a random fact my mind
turns over in its hands every once in a while,

no doubt asking *and why are we keeping this?*
With her tongue, she's working her loose front

tooth, the one that's held on so long it's safe
to call stubborn. If I were wise, I would say

from the driver's seat that I love her like
three hearts, tell her *I wish for extra arms.*

Could I have suction cups, too? The better
to hold on, stay attached, like her baby teeth

want to do. Could we swim in an ocean—
so deep we're out of the light. Out of sight.

I might say *we could be sea creatures with
our extra arms*—tentacles—right. *Tentacles,*

not arms. Our tentacles & extra hearts, together
in our oddness—octopus—octopuses, *octopi.*

A *tangle*—more trivia hoarding in my mind.
We could be so ourselves in our strangeness

that women on the surface driving minivans
to summer camp pause & consider, as they

shift to park, collect the backpacks, ready
the goodbyes, just how wonderous it is to be *us.*

Grocery List as a Love Letter

1.

Standing in the aisle empty-handed,
I envision the list languishing on the counter
back home. I would have sworn I had folded

it in half, would have testified
to feeling its thin skin in my back pocket.
But no.

2.

Then I wonder if I lost it on the way
to the store, and I think of all the places
grocery lists of the past have gone:

wedged into the cracks of a car seat,
dropped in the parking lot like a chewed-up
piece of bubble gum.

Or did the breeze take it?

3.

Once, a grocery list of mine journeyed
in an envelope all the way
to my grandmother's farm,
leaving her to wonder

why I was asking after her health,
then demanding
milk
eggs
butter
flour
bread.

4.

They do read a bit like random notes:

Give me the sugar or else.
We are almost out of coffee creamer,
low on cornmeal and kosher salt.
OATMEAL in all caps

because we can't disappoint the little ones at home.
Extra apples.

Also, I need cocoa.

5.

I have
dire, undeniable needs.
These are my desires.

6.

Milk chocolate.
Peanut butter—smooth.
White wine.

Good tea.

7.

Once, someone told me
even if you leave
the list at home, it will be
easier to remember
what you want
if you've made a list at all;

the act of writing helps
to cement things
in your memory.

8.

I think they were right.
I think I am thankful
I wrote it all down.

9.

A list is not gone only when
you can no longer see it or touch it
or feel it against your skin.

A list still exists even if you
never see it again.

10.

A list is everything
you believe you need
at the time,

and only
as good
as how honest
you were when
you made it.

Resignation

I.

There's a wind that gives an honest rustling to all
the leaves I was meant to rake Sunday.

Brown and maroon, they huddle by the drain, holding on
to the vestiges of the last thunderstorm.

Instead, in the late arc of that afternoon, I laid
my tools down in the yard and said yes to the patch of grass

by the blue Adirondacks.

II.

The hound has long ago
uncovered the secret of life

in the grand patch of sun on the deck, and looks at me
now like I've finally understood the only

lesson he was trying to teach me.

III.

When did all this get so overwhelming, I thought—
not the work of it, not the chores per se but—

I don't know. What's the right word for the fullness
of it all? The realness? The heaviness of their needs,

their voices, insistent demands? The thud of their bodies climbing
on me—the babies, I mean, who are no longer babies, but small

sticky planets that orbit so endlessly, bruising my shins, pulling
my hair, roiling over each other in a contest to be closest to me.

IV.

The attempt to attach the right word to parenting boomeranged
me back to Earth, and what I had at first taken as

half a dozen ants rendezvousing on my arm turned out to be
my son's curly hair tickling my skin.

V.

From the deck, the hound thumps his approval three times.

VI.

Here is my stickiest baby, my son. Here is the shooting star

who never stops moving. He'd come to find me, to lay
with me in the grass. He'd come to lay on my worries.

He'd put all his weight on the invisible list of things
I'd never get done. He'd come to make sure I studied

the bright hazel orbs of his eyes.

Notes on the Poems

1. "You Were Moving" started as a poem in response to *The Atlantic*'s #AtlanticPoetryChallenge in April of 2020 when we were just realizing this pandemic thing might hang around for a while.

2. Similarly, "May 25, 2020" came about a week after the murder of George Floyd in Minneapolis, when much of the world felt heavy and untenable.

3. "We use skin" is a mirror poem, inspired by former U.S. Poet Laureate Tracy K. Smith's "I Sit Outside in Low Late-Afternoon Light to Feel Earth Call to Me" (*The New Yorker*, September 28, 2020).

4. Grand Rapids artist Benjamin Boss's paintings inspired three poems: "Reveal"; "Flourish"; and "After a Storm".

5. C.S. Lewis's *A Grief Observed* (1961) provides the epigraph for "Summer as a map".

6. The epigraph from "The News of the World" comes from Henry Scott Holland's "Death Is Nothing At All" (1910).

7. I hope "If you are alone" does justice to my reading of the late Galway Kinnell's poem "Wait", originally published in *Mortal Acts, Mortal Words* (1980). I think about that poem all the time.

Acknowledgments

I have a tremendous amount of gratitude to express to all the people who have propelled me forward for a number of years. *After the 8-Ball* is my first full-length poetry collection, and holding it in my hands is a dream I started dreaming a really long time ago.

To my parents, Jim and Janet Farrow: I'm already at a loss for words. You put up with a moody teenager who buried her nose in *Jane Eyre* and *The Bell Jar*, disappeared to libraries for hours at a time, crashed Walter the family Oldsmobile (sorry again), and once called you from Ireland crying. You've always supported my deepest passion and encouraged me to keep dreaming big dreams. There aren't adequate words to say thank you for what a gift and a kindness that is.

Mandy. It's pretty handy to have a big sister. It's like being born with a built-in best friend.

I am indebted to my experiences with Michigan State University's English Department. I had the immense privilege of studying under the talented poets Anita Skeen and Diane Wakoski, as well as the wonderful and generous Marcia Aldrich and Gordon Henry. Dr. Skeen was my thesis adviser; I learned so much from her brilliance and patience.

Additionally, many years ago, I had the good fortune of being a part of the MSU Writing Center. There I met and learned from Ninna Roth and Stephanie Sheffield. It's pretty critical (I think) as a woman to meet kick-ass women when you're around the age of twenty.

Here in Grand Rapids, I owe a big part of my heart to the 2013 Lake Michigan Writing Project: Lindsay Ellis, Kari Reynolds, as well as all my colleagues—Lisa Palczewski, Greg Schreur, Rachel Lutwick-Deaner, David Theune, and Rori Meyer, in particular. If I recall, I once made you listen to an essay about Meat Loaf's lasting influence on my adolescence?

To my writerly friends and colleagues in West Michigan: Melissa Fox, Heather Edwards, Jessie Richter, Aric Davis, Steve Assarian, Jo Ellyn Clarey, Jen Andrew, Julie Tabberer, Tim Gloege, and Will Miner. Chris Belding: thank you for your kindness and your example.

Thank you Phillip Sterling! You have always been so generous with your time and support. Thank you Kristin Brace. I try to follow your example of eloquence and grace. Thank you Linda Nemec Foster for your encouragement as well, and for reviewing this book.

Thank you to the Kalamazoo Friends of Poetry and Elizabeth Kerlikowske. Thank you, Elizabeth, for reviewing the book, too!

Todd Kaneko and Amorak Huey: thank you both so much for your kind words on this manuscript.

I am indebted to Dr. Ross Tangedal and the staff of the University of Wisconsin-Stevens Point's Cornerstone Press. Thank you to editorial director Kala Buttke and the editorial staff: Grace Dahl, Cale Jacoby, Angela Green, Pachia Moua, Rosie Acker, Camila Freund, Rhiley Block, and Brett Hill. Thank you, also, to production director Amanda Leibham for the cover design. They did a wonderful job with this book.

There are others I wish to thank. I hope you know how grateful and lucky I am.

Thank you, Micah Alles. Every writer needs a partner who installs a lock on a door for the express purpose of keeping young children at bay. You are always the first person to tell me I can do something.

Lastly, there's a deep amount of gratitude I feel for all the editors and readers of all the magazines who take interest in my work. Gratefully acknowledged are the publishers and editors of the followng magazines, journals, and books, where particular poems first appeared:

"Phases" originally appeared in *Hyype* (Issue 8, 2022); "Haunted" and "The River Liffey" were included as part of the Fall 2021 Decameron Writing Series (Cycle Five); "You don't know" took third place in the Chancellor's Prize, part of the Poetry Society of Michigan's annual contest, and was included in the Fall 2021 *Peninsula Poets: Contest Edition*; "A Mercy", "Grief is an item on a menu I don't want", and "Sonnet for 2020" appeared in *Third Wednesday* (Autumn 2021, Volume XIV, Number 4); "Birds by the Attic Slats", "Love Poem #55", "Mourning, although I must say", "Poem of Parting", "Skirmish", "Take a gander", "Till August", and "You Were Moving" originally appeared in *So What to Say to a Bird* (Celery City Press, Kalamazoo Friends of Poetry, 2021); "Daydream", "Finding a rifle under the bed", "The News of the World", and "Possible Scene of an Accident" originally appeared in *Porch Light to the Longshoreman* (Finishing Line Press, 2019); "After a Party" originally appeared in *The 3288 Review* (Autumn 2019, Volume 5, Issue 2); "Root Systems" was included in "Poetry Inspired by Art 2018," an event held at Fountain Street Church in Grand Rapids, Michigan, in collaboration between the Richard App Gallery and Grand Rapids Poet Laureate Marcel "Fable" Price (on exhibition July 17–August 29, 2018).

COLLEEN ALLES is a native Michigander and writer living in West Michigan. Her fiction and poetry have appeared in *The Michigan Poet, Red Cedar Review, Peninsula Poets, The Write Michigan 2016 Anthology*, and elsewhere. Finishing Line Press has published two chapbooks of her poetry. *So What to Say to a Bird* was named as the state winner in the Michigan category for the Celery City Chapbook Contest, hosted by the Kalamazoo Friends of Poetry. Her first novel, *Skinny Vanilla Crisis*, was published in July of 2020.

She is a contributing editor for short fiction at *Barren Magazine*, and when she isn't reading or writing, she's spending time with her family, including a very rowdy but beloved hound, Charlie.